For Rabbi Broude,

With all good wishes—

Lucy Dry
12/27/82

Self-Portrait
with Hand Microscope

Poems ✍ Lucille Day

Berkeley Poets' Workshop and Press ∽ Berkeley, California

My thanks to the editors of the following magazines and anthologies in which some of the poems in this book first appeared: *Berkeley Poetry Review, Berkeley Poets' Cooperative, Blue Unicorn, Colorado State Review, Contemporary Women Poets* (Merlin Press), *Crazy Ladies, Epos, Lookings and Listenings, The New York Times Magazine, Tunnel Road* (J.F.K. University Press), *US 1 Worksheets, Voices Within the Ark: The Modern Jewish Poets* (Avon Books), *Wisconsin Review.*

"Applying for AFDC," "Fifteen," "Neurochemist," and "Reject Jell-O" first appeared in *The Hudson Review.*

This book was funded in part by a grant from the National Endowment for the Arts.

Front cover photograph of Lucille Day by Charles Klein. Electron micrograph of neural folds by Linda Mak.

Cover: Valerie Winemiller

Book Design: Anne Hawkins and Lucille Day

Typesetting: Ann Flanagan Typography, Berkeley, California

For Liana and Tamarind

Contents

I Hatching Turtles

Love is a shadow.
How you lie and cry after it.
Sylvia Plath

The most beautiful and most profound emotion we can experience
is the sensation of the mystical. It is the source of all true science.
Albert Einstein

Biologist in the Kitchen

When the tea kettle whistles
I hear a hundred bushtits
emit tandem calls.

Two gallinaceous birds painted on my cup
must be pheasants,
but the coloring is wrong—
too bright for females,
too dull for males.

Sunlight slips easily
under the eaves. Mycelia
bloom by the sink

and when the crickets start to sing
I think of the click and shimmer
of polished bone
in the Vertebrate Museum, intricate
skeletons poised on racks.

I sip my cut black tea,
longing for wind in the forested skull,
where roots embrace whole cities
and fattened ants hang
upside-down, under the grass.

Dancers

Dance defines movement:
this is how fish
flit and dip in blue light
lacing kelp blades,
a quiver of spines.

And this is how starfish
watched by stalk-eyed crabs
consume the slow urchins.
Anemones open and close
like green hearts; sea worms
roll in the waves.

Watch now, the sea
lifts from its shell-bowl.
The galaxies expand.
Even in the egg slime
four-horned chromosomes
leap, then recede like stars.

Knee-Deep in Sword Ferns

This topiary forest holds
a handful of birds—
a robin, a goldfinch
and two vireos perch
under a blue-glazed
bowl of sky that blisters,
shrinking in a kiln.

A fox squirrel nest,
twig-tucked and plumped
with lichens and mosses,
squats in the fork
of a bay laurel.
Madrone berries dangle,
edible, raw or cooked.

Scaly rootstocks
knit the soil. I stand
knee-deep in sword ferns;
a creek below me undercuts
its bank, an old fear
flowing on the edge
of consciousness.

A tropical knot of sun.
Brown and white fungus
feeding on heartwood.
The past decays.
I'm startled by cawing:
a Steller's jay escapes
in the crackling heat.

The Lab

My snails caress
the planetary stillness,
dropping opaque eggs
to settle among the elements.
Mosquito larvae flicker,
thousands upon thousands
of tiny red tongues
challenging my ignorance.
Nudibranchs wait
to be opened like antique watches,
springs and jewels to be removed
escapement to be lost
center wheel left to rust

Smashed by centrifugation,
dissolved by sulfuric acid,
dissected and electrocuted,
I am unnerved.
The green oscilloscope snakes
hiss at me, and I shrivel.
Yes, I am embryonic here
with globular eyes
and minute opposable thumbs.
But I am not rocked in cozy fluids:
I am a miscarriage
in prickly light,
an uncomfortable landscape.

Neural Folds
For John Teton

The frog embryos spin,
a million tiny skaters
in bright sacs. Soon
neurons will web each body,
spreading fine mesh
through muscle and skin.

First, the neural folds
must fuse. Crest cells
edging a moon-bald field
reach with bulbous arms;
flowing inward, they move
toward each other.

And when they finally meet,
melding together, cell by cell,
there is no explanation:
they know who they are.
I can almost hear them
yammering in strange tongues.

At Point Lobos

Four nuns flap on the beach
and squirrels eat from our hands.
The spindliest pines I've ever seen
grow here—a forest of bird legs.

On the bluffs the cypresses
pose like dancers. We face
the lavender sea, leaning backward.
Slowly, my limbs begin to twist.

A white-crowned sparrow lands
on my thigh. In future years
you might find me on a sea cliff
in wind, stiff, alive.

Song of the Stickleback

His belly undulates.
I am mesmerized
by its redness.

My own belly bulges,
ready to yield, shimmering
like the dusk sea.

My silver
calls him. I arch my back
in a delicate posture.

He responds
with his zig-zag dance
and I follow

to the nest,
carefully placing my nose
inside. He prods

from behind, and the eggs slip—
so many pale jewels
beneath my fins.

Ragged and dull, ready
to drift alone, I leave him
guarding the nest.

Goldfish

Clouds web the horizon.
A woman thinking of spiders
(silk, black widows)
walks barefoot on sand.
Her fingernails are long,
unpainted. Parched veils
sift between her toes.

And the sea beside her
shines with gold rings,
millions of weddings.
The woman kneels, watches
kelp float in champagne
foaming with lace
gowns of drowning brides.

Today she is alone.
Where is her husband?
At home, holding a round
bowl of goldfish.
He speaks to the fish.
He tells them softly
the woman is crazy.

Poem to Give to a Lover

Today, anything goes:
the bay takes a bow when I clap
and birds whistle Bach.
Beads of light roller-skate
above chimneys and roofs.

The air, alive
with pollen grains looking for mates,
insects that glitter like kings,
and germs that bounce
with every breath we take,

moves incessantly
like the tangle of kelp in its water bed
at the end of the pier. The bay
leaps and curls at our feet.
My heart beats faster.

We are seventy percent water:
our proteins, lipids, nucleic acids
and carbohydrates are packaged
in cells of many shapes—
trees, goblets, boxes, ribbons, bells—

surrounded by liquid.
Let's surge and break in ripples!—
in this atmosphere pulsing with light,
where atoms spin in pairs like tiny lovers
and random paths collide.

Fire

Hear the spit and crack
of kindling. We melt
together like flames.
Sparks fly from our mouths.
Cool blue-green flames
enclose us, a lagoon.

In pewter moonlight
let the house set sail,
lit by embers.
While I sleep, love,
bring me incense and gold.

Your body warms me;
mist becoming rain
clatters the roof.
Tomorrow morning poke
amid ashes, touch
the lovely uncharred forms.

Night Windows

Your dining room table rests,
perhaps, on your neighbor's roof;
your paintings now
are huge piano keys
in your favorite cedar.
Relationships and meaning
hover in a gouache,
transparent, suspended in air.

Stare now at the center
of a black mirror.
Quaking bog, how it quivers!
Carnivorous plants
click in the blackness,
peculiar as love.
Try to enter. Sedges
creep inward, your face
grown scaly with moss.

Mud Flats

On the map of my sleep
there is a bay, gaping at low tide—
a sullen grey mouth,
weedy with eelgrass. I walked
out where basket shells

plow the sticky surface.
I heard the sea's Gothic toll.
Gelid water rushed
over my feet, clam holes,
oyster drills, bones.

Red ghost shrimps hid
in burrows. I was enclosed
by the hiss of channels
filling quickly. Sick
of breathing, I dove.

I Am Waiting

By a window filled with leaves,
slashed by jagged
bits of light,
for a man who comes

like worms. Blackness.
The world turns inside out.

Let chalky trees send
branches curling
inward through atmosphere
too dense to breathe.

I will claw my way out
of this nightmare,
rise from bed,

not screaming obscenities,
but delicately—the way
three new fronds

appeared today
among the curled leaves
and old black stems

of the fern I thought
was dead, its life
somehow linked with my own.

And tonight I started
writing my future
in the wet earth, simply
in signs and dreams he can read

some night in remote silence
when I am close
as the nodes firing his heart.

The Abortion

In my green gown I remembered
the moon as a skewed smile,
the precarious tilt of a sailboat
far from the pier.

It seemed I was always alone.
Now, strangely crowded—
twenty-four of us waiting
in a ten-bed ward—
I touched the shoulder
of the dark-haired girl
hunched next to me, crying.

I remembered the shrill
cry of a black-winged bird
I could not name
and the trail of a shooting star
burning to ash.

The seconal did not affect me.
They gave me more, intravenously,
until my knees began to shake.

I could not rest or sleep
that morning amid masked faces,
pain and the nightmarish whir
of a machine in the next room.

In the raw light I remembered
a house with no number,
paint peeling, windows boarded,
the last one on the street
in a dead-end dream.

Cytogenetics Lab

You enter a rat's eye,
round and dark as a cherry
dangling from the optic nerve.

Inside, a network of cells
complicates the terrain,
rivers winding past sugar pines.

Almost any day you can find
a nucleus where a young woman boards
the windows of her home.

Take cover, she calls,
as wind begins to howl
through membranes and chromosomes.

But her house collapses.
Her skull cracks like a geode,
haloed by orange light.

Crystals cling to your clothes.
When the storm dies, you
emerge, unscathed, from the eye.

The Exchange

I don't know why I entered
that house, pink and white,
a Victorian cupcake,
or what I held in the package
so close to my chest.

Why did I sit on the red
velvet sofa? I didn't trust
the stranger, tiny-eyed,
with the grey beard. Light
pierced the high windows.

He took my package, offering
a round box in its place.
I didn't want to trade.
I hated his gift: I hated
the mask of my face.

Halloween Letter

Pregnant again, I sit
at my desk. How do you like
my paper? It's handmade.
As you read this, remember
that evening—the texture
and weight. How long
has it been since we sat
on the bridge? The baby
kicking. You ran
your fingers along my cheek.

Today I am wearing a mask
my mother sent for the party.
A gauzy fabric covers
my face. I tried
to take it off this morning,
remembering you kissed me.
Bits of skin peeled away.
Now I know I'm stuck with
blood on my fingers,
purdah, a second face.

Neurochemist

Past the insectary and deserted labs
I stride. Like boredom and bad dreams,
empty rooms open on either side of me.

In blue jeans and tie-dyed coat I climb
past the boa cage and metal boxes
of rats and mice, smelling of sawdust and crap.

I select a cage containing five pink-eyed
puffs of white fur, and take my scissors—rusted,
blood-stained, and dulled from cutting through bone.

It's the brain I want, with its stellate cells
and elegantly fluted lobes. The mice
know my coarse white gloves. One whiff and they

scramble, squealing, in every direction,
but I grab one around the soft, pulsing belly.
When it writhes, I tighten my grip.

Quickly I cut through the neck and drop
the twitching body into the sink. Blood spurts
as the heart clamps shut. I hold the head,

mouth open, eyes distant, glazed; I prepare
to enter the skull, looking for what fills
that hollow place: mud, quicksand, love.

Tumor

Small and flat,
I inhabit the mind—
a landscape of pale stars
and electric trees,
where mountains fold on fields,
pearl on grey.

I crouch between cells
by the great salt lake
of the lateral ventricle.
All day I hear
the hiss of blood
twisting through tissue.

I begin to sing. I am
a tiny siren
calling the capillaries
to my cove. They come—
red serpents
coiling around me.

Oh how they love me!
Bringing their gifts
of food and nectar. I fatten,
slowly at first,
then faster and faster, until
I am round as a planet.

My cells spread everywhere,
each one a seed of another self,
but the skull closes
over a desert
tangled with old roots.
Sand starts to blow.

Self-Planting Seeds

In the uneven light
they coil and uncoil,
hanging by tails—
pygmy snakes
ready for self-burial.

The air clings
to leaf and skin; the sky
turns violet and wild.
Seeds drop, writhing, and people
with their griefs and gametes
crawl inside to drive
themselves to bedrock.

Inside, it is winter
and silent as frozen soil,
but this
is the stillness of life,
the time to penetrate
each silvery membrane,
find the nuclei of selves.

The sky stretches, hardens,
fades to grey.
Fine threads of rain
loosen feldspars and clay.

When cells start to tumble,
seed coats cracking, maybe one
sleek creature will rise
speaking of winter and blackness,
mitosis, endosperm
and other lives.

Self-Portrait with Hand Microscope
After the Expressionists

The room is red
for the rooms of my heart
and the births of children.
I am the thin lady
(stiff, angular brushstrokes)
in denim and silk.

Half my mouth curls
in a cynical grin;
one eye is weeping.
I hold the microscope
between thumb and forefinger
like a silver pen.

Having looked at onion roots
and rats' eyes, I bend
to examine my skin,
its star-burst pattern
cracking slowly,
my man in shadows

where mildew and bread mold
are beaded, intricate.
Earthworms cling
to his heart. O slick
muscle closed like a fist!
I search my mind

for the beat of cilia,
their synchronized dance,
the sudden wings
of a fruit fly,
flickering—movement,
live things.

Sitting Again by This Window

Gold light scattered
on roofs, gold light now
worming through trees.
"The apples are golden,"
she said, "imagine it. . .
their million
gold leaves metal and breathless."

> *I can't remember why*
> *I am here. It is hot,*
> *the window always shut.*
> *Again the silence*
> *I breathe overwhelms me.*
> *Dreams of him cool*
> *in my bones; emptiness*
> *grows, stark as a rat's eye.*

White clothesline cords
hang in parabolas, just
outside the window.
The many-angled fence
borders a balding lawn.
Bodega Bay at low tide:
I crossed its surface,
a dull expanse, pockmarked,
patchy with eelgrass.

> *What about visions?*
> *The Cambrian Sea, surrounded*
> *by flutes, the world as*
> *a multicolored eye,*
> *creatures clacking—*
> *chattering rapids of light.*

When I watch long enough,
spiny cushion plants
and bluebunch wheatgrass
grow from my optic nerve.

I love words.
They are stacked in twos.
They are tucked in trees.
They glisten with orange lichen.
They draw bats.

The TV says, ''I am writing
an interview with myself.''
The radio twanging,
''Dreams of crystal streams . . .
far away from where . . .
apples in the evening.''

I wake or sleep. Time
expands to multiply dreams
I cannot touch.
My memories become
seasons too distant to hear.
I listen. I looked for
mirrors of rain
setting fire to clouds,
the cold glow of love.

There were no clouds.
I was naked, bending
in afternoon light.
The bed shimmered.

I turn my head slowly, see
reptiles, birds and mammals
curled in drawers,
enormous metal boxes holding
ponds and river valleys,
my lover—a stately array.

Blue light, they say,
is round, secret,
deep at high tide. I
sometimes think corneal cells
are continents in blue dye,
where my pale eyes hold
chromosomes, mitoses.

Three black pines keep
vigil on the streetlit sky—
pinkish grey,
swollen with clouds.

I hold my face
in my hands, remember
bogs and old fields beyond
the window, the language
of dry paper turning brown.
Night turns instinctively
in the clockwork light.
I close my eyes, fingertips
grazing lips; I can't
remember my face.

Hatching Turtles

Three feet under the surface
green turtles hatch.
They emerge, flippers beating,
covered with sand.

> There is a gallery with red
> wall-to-wall carpets.
> In the gallery are black paintings
> and black paintings only.

The turtles, dark, identical,
scoot across the beach.
Frigate birds swoop
to grab them, one by one.

> More black pictures:
> stone houses
> with no doors or windows,
> shadows of bone.

Crisscrossed by shadows
of claws, they struggle
against the clamor of wings.
They must reach the sea.

> The season is winter.
> Each person receives a number.
> An even number means ''home,''
> an odd one, ''execution.''

The turtles climb up dunes.
They are too slow!
The water surrounds one,
cold, unexpectedly cold.

The dream is cold as Siberia.
It is not safe. The dangerous air
pierces my lungs. There is
no haven, no safe dream.

II Changing Trains

> . . . *one night during the long*
> *Intensity of your observation, you look so perfectly*
> *That you finally see yourself, off in the distance*
> *Among the glittering hounds and hunters, beside the white*
> *Shadows of the swans.*
>
> Pattiann Rogers

The Gambler's Daughter

Before I knew my ABCs I learned to deal.
I performed at Daddy's Friday night
poker parties. I got to stay up late,
a good thing: I was afraid of the dark.
Sometimes, alone in my room, I saw the nights
as a deck of cards, stacked against me.

On Sundays Daddy and I fed the ducks
at Lake Merritt. Mallards scrambled for crumbs.
Swans drifted past the caged bald eagle.
Canada geese everywhere. Their calls
mingled with the bells from Our Lady of Lourdes,
and coots swam in pools of orange light.

I learned to read the handicaps when I was six.
I picked Lover's Dream and Lucky Lucy,
and Daddy took my bets downtown to the bookie
with his and Mama's. Mama and I sat
on her bed, beside the radio, fingers crossed.
She gave me fifty cents whenever she won.

At Steinhart Aquarium Daddy and I saw
batfish, flat, shaped like fans with yellow
tails and fins. Their eyes, black-banded,
twitched while they swam, mouths small pink slits,
opening and closing as they came toward me,
my hand in Daddy's, my nose pressed to the glass.

I looked into their eyes, liking them
better than the rockfish or eels, better
even than Ulysses, the bug-eyed bass.
They seemed to have a message for me
that I couldn't decode. I watched, wondering
if they knew what I knew: they were trapped.

I got my first jackpot when I was seven,
at the Cal-Neva Club just before breakfast.
Daddy shooed me back to the table. I could
hardly swallow my pancakes. He came back
with a red plastic cup filled with nickels
and a stack of keno tickets for me to mark.

I pretended I was the only daughter
of the Brownings or Curies, though there were no
books of poetry or science in our house.
Mama read *TV Guide, Modern Screen*
and *True Confessions;* Daddy read *Playboy,*
murder mysteries and science fiction.

I was never very popular with the kids
at school, though I taught them how to play
spit in the ocean, California poker,
lowball and five-card stud. I kept an extra ace
up my sleeve, but I rarely used it. I learned
to take chances; I knew how to bluff.

I Wanted a Baby

More than anything that Christmas Eve
in my room, sunlight easing through the windows,
my parents out at a party, I wanted a baby
with Bill, who didn't complain
when I kept getting up to check the blood.

Black sheath crumpled around my waist,
eyes shut, I tried to concentrate on names:
Aaron, Eric, Priscilla, Adela.
Bill pressed his lean body against mine
and whispered, ''Are you sure it's safe?''

Every day, I woke up hoping to be sick
and dressed in baggy clothes for practice.
My mother marveled at my glow.
Beneath my bed my eighth grade texts rested,
scorned as the stones in my yard.

Now, amazed by muted reds and greys,
limestone and clay in bands that remember
the sea, I remember how people smiled
at me in particular, a real person
at last, with my imaginary child.

First Wedding

If the sky that day had opened not its blue room,
but its grey one, and we had been wed
rain-drenched in Reno, thunder cracking,
it wouldn't have mattered. But the sun was out
to brighten the walls of the old stone church.

All the dolls were long dead by then,
cold and waxy in cribs and shoe box beds,
dust collecting like memories.
I was fourteen, wearing new white shoes
and my blue-flowered satin Chinese dress.

Frank was three years older, looking skinny
in his rented suit. Our mothers asked the organist
to play "I Love You Truly," and they crooned
and wept. I pretended it was "Love Me Tender."
The men were silent. My father bowed his head.

Standing at the altar, I remembered my blue room.
For years the walls had been shrinking.
I saw myself grown huge like Alice
in a box, small and blue, the door shrunken
to shoe box size. I had to burn my way out.

Now, in the cool light of the sanctuary
all my wounds were soothed. Frank was smiling.
It was hard not to giggle, saying "I do,"
and when we knelt I thought my dress would rip,
but it held, and my hand grew heavy with diamonds.

Afterwards we went outside for pictures
to put in our white and gold vinyl book.
We stood under leaves, before a wall of stone,
and now I stare at the girl in the blue Chinese dress.
O child behind my mirror, smiling, trapped.

Fifteen

I was pregnant that year,
stitching lace and purple-flowered ribbon
to tiny kimonos and sacques.
I still thought sperm
came out like pollen dust in puffs of air.

I ate cream of wheat for breakfast, unsalted,
diapered a rubber doll
in my Red Cross baby care class, and sold
lipsticks and gummy lotions to housewives
to pay for a crib.

Oh, it was something, giving birth.
When my water bag splattered
I screamed, and the neat green anaesthesiologist
said, "Why don't you shut up?"
"Fuck you!" I shrieked.

"Breathe deep," was the last thing
I heard him say.
Ten minutes later I woke up.
The obstetrician with his needle and thread,
busy as a seamstress,

winked at the pink-haired nurse
who brought me my baby girl,
wrinkled and howling.
"She's lovely. I'd like a cheeseburger
and milkshake now," I said.

Reject Jell-O

The man I married twice—
at fourteen in Reno, again in Oakland
the month before I turned eighteen—
had a night maintenance job at General Foods.
He mopped the tiled floors and scrubbed
the wheels and teeth of the Jell-O machines.
I see him bending in green light,
a rag in one hand,
a pail of foamy solution at his feet.
He would come home at seven a.m.
with a box of damaged Jell-O packages,
including the day's first run,
routinely rejected, and go to sleep.
I made salad with that reject Jell-O—
lemon, lime, strawberry, orange, peach—
in a kitchen where I could almost touch
opposing walls at the same time
and kept a pie pan under the leaking sink.
We ate hamburgers and Jell-O
almost every night
and when the baby went to sleep
we loved, snug in the darkness pierced
by passing headlights and a streetlamp's gleam,
listening to the Drifters and the Platters.
Their songs wrapped around me
like coats of fur, I hummed in the long shadows
while the man I married twice
dressed and left for work.

Applying for AFDC

I sat in the Welfare Office
in nylons and spike-heeled shoes,
hair stacked to make my height
between six-two and six-four.

I wore a tight black sleeveless dress,
a black eyeliner mole
on my right cheek, and a gold
snake bracelet coiled on my upper arm.

A woman in tennis shoes and a red muumuu
who'd been waiting all morning
cursed the girl at the desk.
A small boy yelled, ''Right on!''

Social workers frowned in all the doorways.
I chain-smoked Marlboros
and paced the floor. Changing
my baby's diapers for the third time

in the restroom, I noticed my shadow—
a flat lady, cringing in the corner.
The gaudy one in the mirror grimaced at me.
You'd think I owed them something—these
strangers I'd rather ignore.

Amelia Davis

Almost ninety now, she has lived
with her plants in fir-panelled rooms
this past half-century,
watching neighbors come and go.
At first her life seems distant, subtle
as a landscape in a Chinese painting—

a solitary woman, stooped
by a river laced with delicate waves.
Then you hear a piano: her fingers
remember hymns and ragtime tunes.
Her house rings. "Rock of Ages."
I listen outside when she plays.

Her only child died at five.
His pictures fade into walls,
deep wood, the past she would enter
if it weren't for the towhee
piping now, the buds on the plum tree,
the children by the creek.

My Grandma Emma had eight children,
all born in a farmhouse.
She died of pneumonia in 1918.
Grandma Ada died when I was four.
We used to cut out paper dolls,
her orange cat named Oscar curled at our feet.

No one's Grandma, Amelia walks
up and down the block;
she invites her neighbors over for sherry.
They seldom accept. She dreams
she is still a young woman
with long brown hair and a plump baby.

Labor

All night the Shabbos candles
beat like twin hearts.
I awoke every hour
and when they finally went out
I got up.
It was still dark.

Now, clouds blister the sky—
a terrible rash, all white.
The sun is no poultice,
but the wind
soothes and soothes.

Soon the pain will be over.
I am going to find a room.
It will be all white
except for my blood
and one lamp
burning like a small sun.

I will not notice it.
Cool drafts will cover my body.
Outside, the sky will clear.
By noon
someone will be born.

Woman in Blue Jeans and Wool Socks

She dusts the copper sugar bowl
and fills the garlic pot
before starting supper. Each
teaspoon leveled, she folds
flour and white batter
into butter, eggs, vanilla
and sugar, creamed.

Coffee cake safe in the oven,
chicken simmering in olive oil
and wine, she takes a razor blade
and scrapes paint from doors,
window frames and walls,
exposing the dark wood beneath.

In every cottage there is a woman
dusting floral china,
arranging a table with bowls
of strawberries and cream.

In every heart there is a question
of fruit and honey, razor blades
and wood like dark water,
the swirling grain.

Paint chips fly in the woman's face
and catch beneath her nails.
Trees glisten in the first fall rain;
creeks that were shallow in summer
churn and rise.

Coffee cake burns in the oven.
Chicken boils over in olive oil and wine.
Something rises inside the woman,
sharp, a knife, a cry.

Housework

Pinkish nodules on the plum tree,
the first white blossoms
already a pandemonium of bees.
New leaves crown
the buckeye meristems, the yard
bathed in a buttery gleam.

A fine day to be outdoors,
but Mama spends her day off
helping me with housework,
her specialty. She still
has to do this for a living
five days a week.

"Next time you better get a man
with money," she warns,
shaking her dust rag.
"Is this the life for you and me?"

I don't know, Mama.
Winters come and go, the children
outgrowing their warm clothes,
the moon covered with clouds
or polished to a high sheen.

The vacuum cleaner hums
in all the corners, sucking
cobwebs from ceiling beams.
At seventeen I thought someday
I'd hire someone to clean *her* house,
send Dad and her to Europe.
I still have an unsnapped picture
of them on a cruise in Germany—
terraced vineyards and a white castle
rising in the background.

Today the daffodils nod,
oblivious, drunk on the thick light
striking the mirrors
smudged with handprints
for Mama and me to clean.
Dark cows cluster
on the green banks of the Rhine.

Mama, I'd like to write a poem
you could fly on.
Mama, look at that fuzzy spider
hovering above the TV.

Patterns
For Liana

A lacework of leaf shadows,
small flames of light
on a wall, patterns
changing and changing.
I wish all boundaries
could give way so easily
as I watch you struggling
into womanhood.

Did I ever tell you
that a woman is born twice,
that the first
person she gives birth to
is herself?

I have shown you all I know
of snow and summer,
of empty cups and the cellar
filled with wine,
of knives and fine silk
and dead trees and living.

I have pointed out Orion,
sword ferns, pines,
and red-winged blackbirds,
and held you close all night
beside the pivoting sea.

I reach for you now
but am burned
by a light too intense
to watch or hold.

I sit alone, but see
your face streaked with light

changing, faster and faster.
You, too, are alone
in a small boat,
rowing. Push, push—
I'm waiting for you
and when you arrive I want
to be the first to know.

Nature Poems

Oh, I still see the squirrels prance
on oak branches, then leap
to my neighbor's roof, tails thrashing.

But my daughter, sixteen last summer,
has a thirty-year-old lover
with tattooed arms
and a weak heart. He rides
a Harley, ponytail flying,
and wears a black leather vest.

I want to write subtle things
about plum leaves the color of wine
and the old women
who live alone on my street.

I want to drink Mocha Java coffee
in my blue kimono on an antique divan.

I want to fall asleep
holding a book of poems instead of a man,
but I keep worrying my daughter's lover
will have a heart attack in bed.

I want to write about the wild roses,
their loud skirts
opening for the sun, but some things

beautiful are dangerous—the way
a young woman's heart
blooms so lavishly,
red plush, over the knife
on a road glittering in moonlight,
when fear is enough.

Letting Go

When you jump with a parachute,
everything tiny and far away
When you leave your childhood
When you slide from the turntable
in the funhouse, you have no control.
Letting go of your dreams,
you feel lighter, careening
toward some other destination.
You must let go of your children.
They were never really yours.
And your life, that uncomfortable suit,
a little too tight, with the odd
pattern you never could figure out
and the fabric that was clearly wrong.

Quilt

Moving through a tunnel
at tremendous speed, you'll see
a quilt bordered with coffins.
The square in the center
is a cemetery plot; with each
family death a coffin
is moved to the center.
A bright spot at the end.
You'll separate from your body,
meet your friends. You can't
come back if you pass the gate
at the end of the path.
I want to move the coffins
back to the border, push
people back through the gate
and in the center quilt a tree.
I want to make the quilt
where the beggar woman,
bent, covered with sores,
rises from the floor
of the bus depot in Tel Aviv,
young and slender
with thick black hair,
and disappears with her ticket
in the dazzling heat.

Inside the Pine Cones

In my great-great grandfather's
castle on the Rhine
all the ancestors surround me,
offering knockwurst.
I say, *I'm Jewish.*
They say, *We'll hide you.*

*

On a street corner in Tel Aviv
I want to speak,
but the alien syllables
stick in my throat—
fish bones. Something
explodes nearby. When I try
to scream, whole fish
slide from my mouth.

*

When the bomb blast cut
a two-inch hole in the pipeline,
black ants crawled out
to play on the frozen tundra.

*

The plane was hijacked
to Las Vegas. The terrorists
played keno all afternoon.
They took a slot machine along
with them to Cuba.

*

One and a half hours by bus
from Tel Aviv to Jerusalem.
Not a camel, donkey,
or grain of sand in sight,
just pinkish stony land
dotted with conifers.

Someone says, *Where are
the angels?* I say,
Inside the pine cones.
                    *

Armies of black ants
stalk the sand on stilts.
By day they're benign.
At night they grow large,
take to the air
and drop bombs. Ships sink
quickly; the Rhine maiden
says Kaddish.

Yom Kippur

Kol Nidre

This is a symphony—the long
melodious chant of swallows
that rise sunward, beating
like a thousand hearts.
They sing of the wound
and blood's dark tendrils,
of the hidden nest
and the slow healing.
They land in a field
of blue flowers
as darkness unfolds
and cold stars settle.

Torah

Two goats. One
is to be sacrificed:
straight bones and firm
muscles will burn.
The other receives the sins
of the people, goes free.
The burden twists him;
skin and muscles rip.
He wanders alone, blind,
edging into dusk.

Ne'ilah
Again the day rolls
into darkness; the sky
spills its pinks and purples,
draining to blackness. Deep
inside there is a closing,
a small gate
swinging shut in the mind.
Those few last thoughts
rush through, and a life
is sealed. Beyond the meadow
a lone bird sounds its call,
waits for response.

Changing Trains

We are changing trains
in the middle of the night,
those of us who knew
it was time to get off.

The country is foreign,
the unfamiliar air grows thick
with insects that glisten metallically.

We are changing trains,
our hot bodies pressed so close
I can scarcely move.

My throat is dry, a desert
spreading inside me.

Black hills in the distance
rimmed with stars, spiked
like the cells of the brain,

we are changing trains
and a strange man
hands my suitcase to the conductor,
whose face is dark and radiant.

I look back once, too late to return.
Sand covers the prints
of a desert bird.

Fingers of light from the coach
push back the darkness,
pulling me forward
toward a mapless country.
I climb on board.

Lucille Day works as a technical writer, free-lance writer, and math/science education consultant. She holds an M.A. in zoology and a Ph.D. in science and mathematics education, both from the University of California, Berkeley. *Self-Portrait with Hand Microscope,* her first collection of poems, received the Joseph Henry Jackson Award.

Books from the Berkeley Poets' Workshop and Press

Berkeley Poets Cooperative Anthology, 1970-1980, poetry & fiction, 256 pages, $6.95.

Snake Blossoms by Belden, poetry & fiction, 64 pages, $3.00.

Jackbird by Bruce Boston, fiction, 88 pages, $3.00.

She Comes When You're Leaving by Bruce Boston, fiction, 64 pages, $3.00.

Slow Juggling by Karen Brodine, poetry, 48 pages, $3.00.

Seaward by Betty Coon, poetry, 44 pages, $3.00.

Unfree Associations by Michael Covino, poetry, 60 pages, $3.95.

Newspaper Stories by Patricia Dienstfrey, poetry, 36 pages, $3.75.

All Pieces of a Legacy by Charles Entrekin, poetry & fiction, 54 pages, $3.00.

Casting for the Cutthroat by Charles Entrekin, poetry, 40 pages, $3.95.

Half a Bottle of Catsup by Ted Fleischman, poetry, 40 pages, $3.00.

Hear My Story by Dennis Folly, poetry, 48 pages, $3.95.

The Ghost of the Buick by Bruce Hawkins, poetry, 54 pages, $3.95.

Wordrows by Bruce Hawkins, poetry, 40 pages, $3.00.

Wash Me on Home, Mama by Peter Najarian, fiction, 84 pages, $3.00.

Once More Out of Darkness by Alicia Ostriker, poetry, 32 pages, $3.00.

John Danced by Gail Rudd, poetry, 40 pages, $4.00.

Over by the Caves by Jennifer Stone, fiction, 64 pages, $3.00.

The Machine Shuts Down by Rod Tulloss, poetry, 40 pages, $3.95.

B·P·W·P
BERKELEY
·POETS·
WORKSHOP
& PRESS
P.O. Box 459
Berkeley, CA 94701